06/02 aug 7.95

D0375280

Fly Casting for Everyone

Other books by Marnie Reed Crowell

Greener Pastures

North to the St. Lawrence

Great Blue, The Odyssey of a Heron

Rainbow Catcher

199.12
LEW

Fly Casting
for Everyone

Gary Lewis
Fly Fishing Program Director and Guide
Lone Mountain Ranch
Big Sky, Montana

with Marnie Reed Crowell
and Peter H. McNair

STACKPOLE
BOOKS

Canon City Public Library
Canon City, Colorado

Copyright © 1996 by Gary Lewis, Marnie Reed Crowell,
Peter H. McNair, and Robert Spannring

Published by
STACKPOLE BOOKS
5067 Ritter Road
Mechanicsburg, PA 17055

All rights reserved, including the right to reproduce this book or por-
tions thereof in any form or by any means, electronic or mechanical,
including photocopying, recording, or by any information storage and
retrieval system, without permission in writing from the publisher. All
inquiries should be addressed to Stackpole Books, 5067 Ritter Road,
Mechanicsburg, PA 17055.

Printed in the United States of America

10 9 8 7 6 5 4 3 2 1

First edition

Illustrations by Robert Spannring
Cover design by Caroline Miller

Library of Congress Cataloging-in-Publication Data

Lewis, Gary.
    Fly casting for everyone / Gary Lewis with Marnie Reed Crowell
and Peter H. McNair : illustrations by Robert Spannring.
        p.   cm.
    ISBN 0-8117-2525-1 (pbk.)
    1. Fly casting. I. Crowell, Marnie Reed II. McNair, Peter H.
III. Title
SH454.2.L48   1996
799. 1'2—dc20   95-37129
                                                         CIP

Preface

Given both a new fly rod and a book about fly casting, probably every fisherman on earth will pick up the fly rod first. It is
also true that he or she will not be satisfied with those first
casts. So pick up the book now. Keep the fly rod handy, and
use both the book and the rod as you work through this guide.

We all have twenty-nine bones in each arm, but we are not
all built alike. We each have our own style of doing things.
What style will work for you? Casting is a subtle art, but it
is not difficult. Here are five steps that will teach you to cast
elegantly and efficiently no matter what size and shape you
are. Try to fix in your mind the simple sequence for casting
correctly. Get the flow of the cast in your mind and muscle
memory. Then when you are ready to review, you will find
some casting tips. You will learn to be your own coach.

Happy casting!

Canon City Public Library
Canon City, Colorado

Getting Started

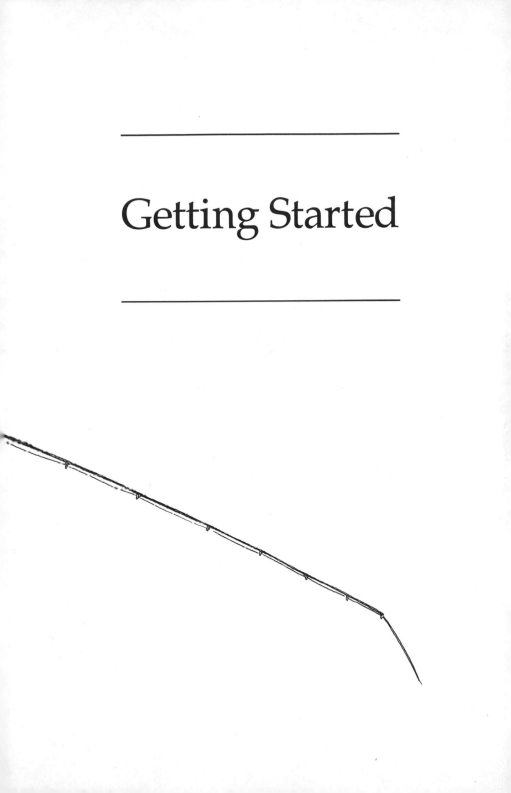

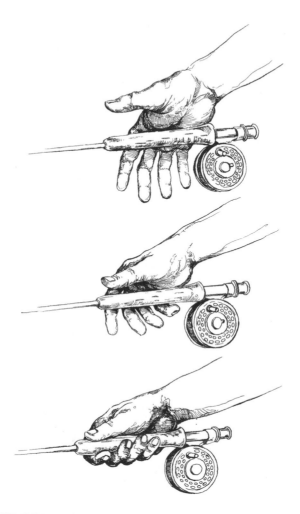

THE GRIP

How is your hand built? Reach out as though you are going to shake hands. Your thumb will point in the direction of your intended target. Shake hands with the rod grip. Your thumb will naturally fall very close to being on top of the rod grip. Whether it lies exactly on top or somewhat around to the side depends on how your hand is engineered. Search for what feels comfortable.

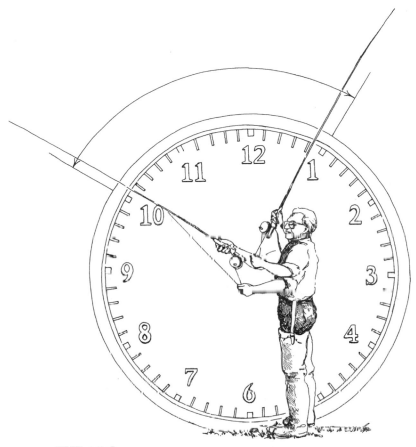

THE ARC

Picture the hands on a clock face. Twelve o'clock is directly overhead. Ten o'clock is out in front of you. One o'clock is just behind you. With no line on the rod, try bringing the rod back to a one o'clock position. Stop your arm as soon as you see the rod passing by your face. Now bring the rod forward to ten o'clock. You have described an arc of 90 degrees between ten and one o'clock.

When you look at pictures of casters from any angle, always think of the ten o'clock position as being in front of the caster.

THE STANCE

Place your feet about the same width apart as your shoulders. Try placing the foot opposite your rod hand slightly forward. Line yourself up so that this foot points toward the target to which you'd like to cast. Does that feel balanced to you? Some people put the rod foot—the foot on the same side as the casting arm—forward for close targets, and the line foot—the foot on the side where the free hand holds the line—forward for distant ones. Whichever foot you put forward, face the target, and take a balanced, comfortable position.

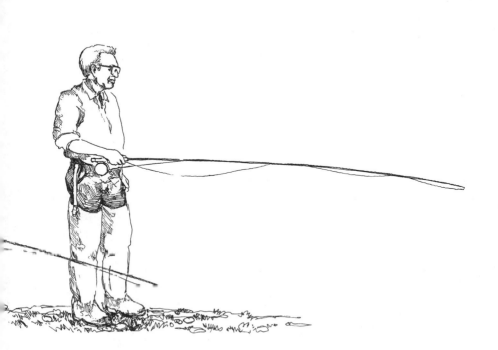

*Take a position that feels comfortably
balanced to you.*

THE CAST

Put down a target, such as a Frisbee, about two or three rod lengths away, something less than 25 feet. Now lay out the line along the ground from the target back to your standing place. This is the distance you want to learn to cast. You will have to put the rod down to do this. If you are outside take care not to get sand in the reel. Put something such as your hat or bandanna on the ground and set the rod butt and reel on that.

THE COUNT

We divide the cast into a count of five. Having a clear mental picture of each step will help you learn much more quickly. Understanding and muscle memory will help you make good casts. As a mnemonic device, say the following to yourself as you go through each step: ON TRACK, BACK CAST, STOP. PAUSE, FORE CAST, FISH THROUGH.

> ON TRACK (Step 1—Get on track.)
> BACK CAST (Step 2—Pick up. Accelerate.)
> STOP. PAUSE (Step 3—Stop. Hesitate.)
> FORE CAST (Step 4—Forward. Accelerate. Stop.)
> FISH THROUGH (Step 5—Complete presentation and fish it through.)

Keep your attention focused on what you are doing. Casting is a combination of hand, body, and mind. Get into the rhythm totally.

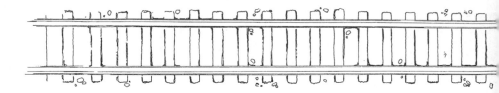

ON TRACK
Step 1. The Preparation
Bring the fly line onto the imaginary track that points to the target. When you are fishing, your line will be out on the water. In that case, step 1 is a gradual, smooth picking up of the line and the leader and getting them in motion. In your practice sessions, the line will be lying out in front of you on the ground or floor. In any case, be certain that the line lies straight in front of you with no slack. That way, when you begin the pickup by raising your rod tip, your line will begin to move as soon as your rod moves. This is important.

Begin step 1 with your rod tip well below your belt and pointing down at the water or ground. Touch the water or ground with your rod tip. This will guarantee that when you pick up, the slack will be minimal. Take up any slack with your free hand just before your rod hand starts to move into the back cast. During the cast you will hold that free hand close against your body, lightly controlling the slack line.

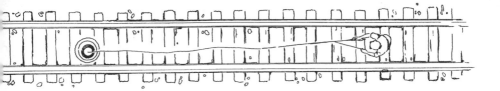

It is very important that you hold the rod tip down.
Then your free hand takes up the slack and you are on
track.

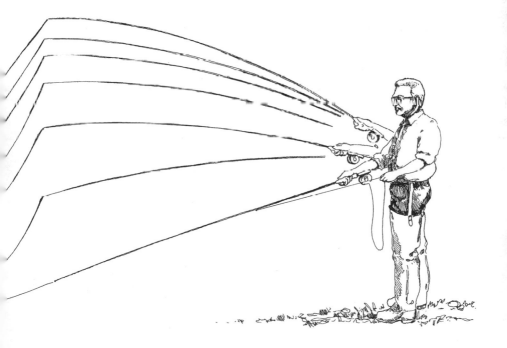

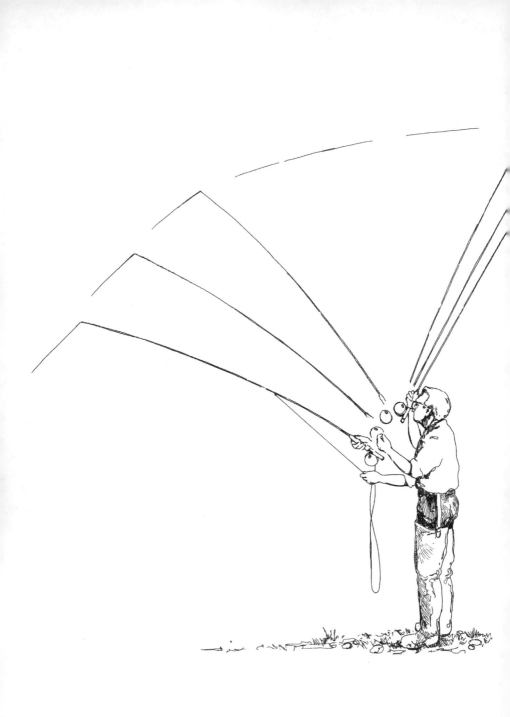

BACK CAST
Step 2. The Back Cast: Pick Up. Accelerate
Now begin the back cast, pulling back the rod by raising your forearm *smoothly*. With a neat, energetic motion, lift your arm, rod, and rod tip up and back to the one o'clock position, near your ear. Your hand is just at the side of your head. Don't put too much wrist action into this stroke. The purpose of the back cast is to lift the line off the water and get it traveling over your head.

Pick up. Accelerate. A neat, contained
motion, the pickup-accelerate gives speed
to your fly line.

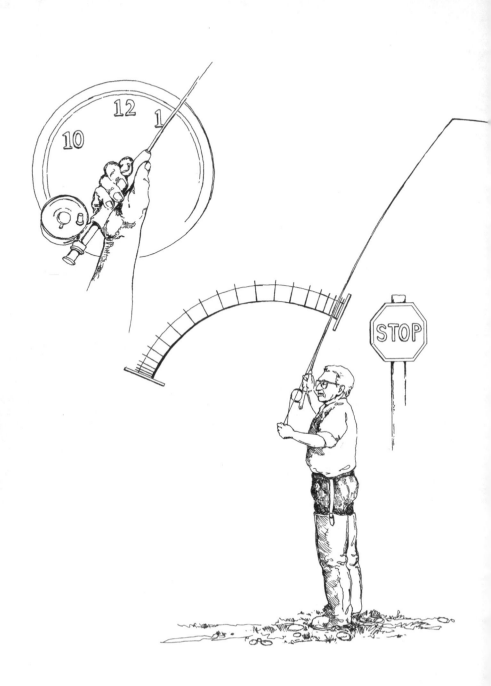

STOP. PAUSE
Step 3. The Pause: Stop. Hesitate
Your wrist will be slightly cocked, and the acceleration of the back cast will cause your wrist to travel a bit farther in a very tiny movement. Stop at one o'clock. This stop is really a slight pause, a hesitation, that has enough energy to be thought of as a *flick*. Picture the briefest spark, an upward stab or lift with the acceleration at the flick. That will help you get the right feeling into your muscle memory.

Stop. Hesitate. If you were to look over your shoulder, you would see the line unfolding in a J or a candy-cane shape, often called the "loop." As your rod tip continues slightly back, you can feel the line "loading," or pulling on the rod.

FORE CAST
Step 4. The Forward Delivery Cast: Forward. Accelerate. Stop
The delivery cast is nearly a mirror image of what you have just done on the back cast. Bring the rod forward with peak acceleration just before your stop at ten o'clock. Usually that is just as your rod tip comes into view. Accelerate, then come to a quick stop.

Those accelerations and abrupt stops bracketing the cast are the key to an efficient cast. You are not throwing your whole arm or shoulder into it, just executing an acceleration with a neat and abrupt stop. You dance the rod back, and you push the rod out in front of you. That forward acceleration when you "commit" needs to be directing the rod tip toward the target you have chosen. Do you still remember there is a target out there?

You undoubtedly have shifted your weight naturally onto your leading foot. You did it so slowly and gradually that you probably did not even realize you were shifting your weight. You just did it. Your knees bent themselves a little to carry you in a nice, springy way. By the time you were ready to deliver that final punch, your body just naturally helped drive the line out.

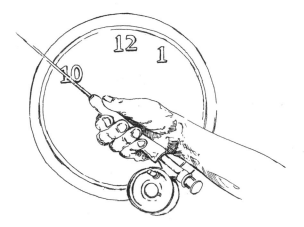

Forward. Accelerate. As you stop and hesitate on the forward cast, you will be aware that the line is traveling rapidly toward your target. Your rod tip lowers slightly as you begin your follow-through.

FISH THROUGH
Step 5. The Follow-through: Complete Presentation and Fish It Through
Your rod tip should be pointing toward your target. Lower the rod tip and point it directly at that spot on the water. Enjoy watching your leader turn over nicely (it lays itself out straight ahead of the end of the fly line). Watch your line settle gently down.

You are not through yet. Your free hand has been near the reel, guiding the line. Now transfer the line promptly with the free hand, tucking it under the middle finger of your rod hand. If it feels better for you to use your index finger, that is fine, but this finger is farther around the rod handle, so it's not our first choice. This light grip on the line with your middle finger allows you to brake by pressing line against the rod handle whenever you need to. With your free hand, you now can take hold of the loose line between your rod hand and the reel and start stripping in line. You are now fishing.

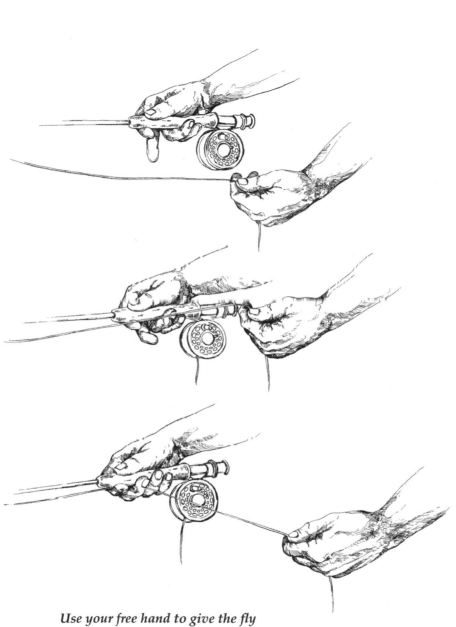

*Use your free hand to give the fly
line to your rod hand.*

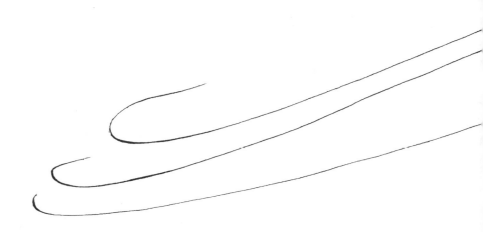

No matter how your cast turns out, always try to follow through. Repeat the entire mnemonic series to yourself: On track, Back cast, Stop. Pause, Fore cast, Fish through. Fish out the cast so you will not cause a disturbance on the water that would alert fish to your presence or miss the strike of the fish that likes the look of the presentation, even though it was not what you intended. When you are practicing, it is sometimes very hard to make yourself wait until you have counted through the five steps. It is tempting to flip your line back into another cast almost before the line settles to the ground or water. *Don't do it!* Take time to visualize a perfect landing on the water. Ask yourself whether you really hit your target. If not, can you determine why you didn't?

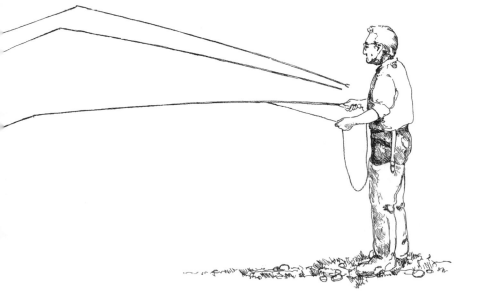

Here's a finished cast, and it looks nearly identical to getting on track.

Casting Tips

Learn to be your own coach. Plan to practice a half hour every day. Don't try to learn fishing and casting all at the same time. If you make learning to cast and learning to fish separate experiences, you will have more fun doing both.

Now go back to page 2. Reread each section, and then apply the following coaching tips. These are helpful suggestions for correcting mistakes. You do not want to form bad habits by making the same mistakes over and over.

It's easier to untangle your lines—and it's much safer—if you practice casting without a fly on your line. Getting snagged by a hook is no fun. When you are fishing, you will want to wear a hat and polarized sunglasses to eliminate glare and help you see fish—the lenses will also protect your eyes from flying hooks. Similarly, a hat and a long-sleeved shirt will protect your skin from both the sun and stray hooks.

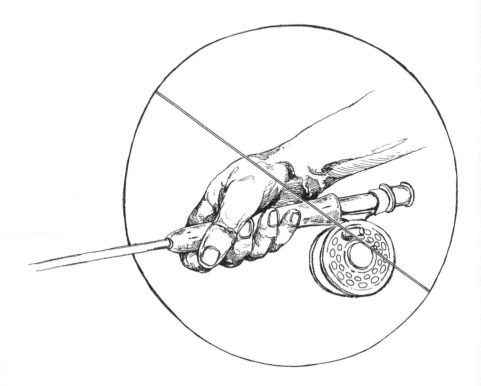

THE GRIP

Aim for a grip with the thumb as nearly on top as is comfortable for you. You may think you want to stretch your index finger along the top of the grip; push back on the rod, and you will feel the stretch that signals that this is not a good position. If you put the V of your thumb and forefinger over the top of the rod, the rod will easily push right up into the V, giving you little control over it and tempting you to "break" your wrist, bending it back too far. Since this will cause you problems, it's important to learn a good grip. If you play tennis or golf, you probably know the feeling of a good grip.

THE ARC

Measure an arc of 90 degrees—the distance on a clock face between ten and one o'clock, a quarter of a circle—and practice against it until you know just what it looks and feels like. For a short cast, this 90-degree arc is all you need. The most common mistake is to take the rod too far back.

See how the rod hand describes the path of the bicycle wheel. Dr. Al Kyte and Dr. Gary Moran did the biomechanics research to determine this by fastening markers on fly casters and videotaping them in front of a grid.

THE IMAGINARY BICYCLE WHEEL

How much of your arm, shoulder, and body should you use? Some people describe a track, running your arm back and forth in one vertical plane. Others describe moving your arm in an arc. Which is it? The casting movement is both. Picture a bicycle wheel with your elbow as the hub and with the rim at the level of your eyes and ears.

Don't just read about the bicycle wheel motion. Try it with your rod in hand. You have to do it to feel it. You have to take time to put the correct motions into your muscle memory so that you can call them up when you want them.

The Rim

Picture your grip as being fastened on the rim of the wheel. Look at the drawing and notice where on the tire rim the reel rests. Place your free hand on the reel and reach back as if you were casting. Feel the imaginary bicycle tire carrying your rod hand in an arc. It rides up the rim from ten o'clock to the twelve o'clock position on the tire and then moves slightly beyond, heading down the clock face to one o'clock, two o'clock, and so on.

The Hub

Now picture the bicycle wheel riding back and forth in a grooved track. The hub—your elbow—rides back and forth just above your waist. The hub of your elbow travels from the handshake position, rides up in back of you, and returns to the handshake position at your belt. Now perform this motion as you send your free hand along for the ride by placing it lightly on the reel. Your free hand will direct you to use the groove and will keep you from flapping your arm out like a turkey wing.

How far back do you let that wheel roll? For a short cast, you don't want the rod to go back farther than one o'clock. As the imaginary bicycle wheel rides back, move your body and shoulder only as much as is necessary for smooth movement, and do not raise your arm too high.

Obviously it will make some difference whether you are male or female and whether your arm is built like that of a weightlifter, a basketball player, or a jockey, but you do not want your upper arm to sneak higher than your shoulder.

START WITH A SHORT LINE

Do not aim for long casts at first. Fishing a long line as a beginner will create problems, and you will not catch many fish. Most fish are caught close to the fisherman, within 15 to 30 feet. Many fish "hold" along the bank, and your long cast may alert them as you cast over them. You will not be able to control a long length of line on the surface of a stream because of intervening currents, and you will have more difficulty feeling and seeing a strike and setting the hook. Trying to cast a long line at first just means that you have more room in which to make mistakes. Ask yourself whether you are casting just to try to look good, or are you trying to catch fish?

We are learning a short, straight line cast—the basic,
beginner's cast. On the water you also will have to think
about how to present your fly without "lining" the fish—
alerting the fish by dropping your line right on top of it.
Think carefully about where you stand to make your
casts. You will disturb the bottom environment less if
you do not wade through it. Fishing from the bank can
be most effective. Anglers often find themselves standing where they really ought to be fishing.

THE STANCE

Get each cast off to a good start by lining up your stance correctly. If you are wading, this may be a challenge. Be certain you are comfortable and balanced.

You don't want any unnecessary twisting. If you see your line falling diagonally across the path to your target, you may be standing incorrectly or you may have a cast of what we'll call the "slanty wobbles."

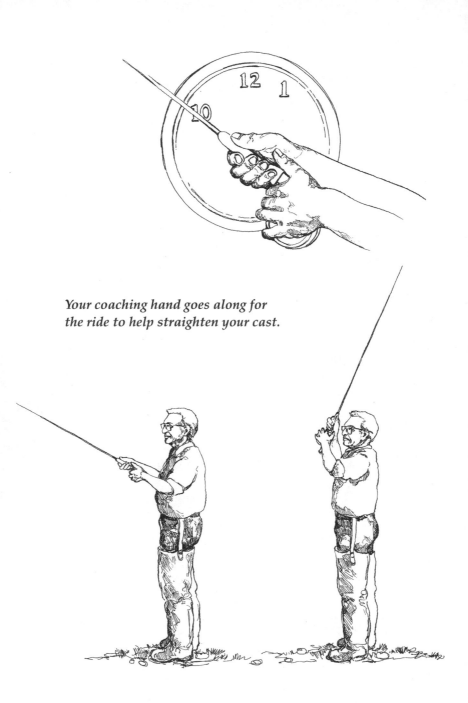

*Your coaching hand goes along for
the ride to help straighten your cast.*

STRAIGHTENING YOUR CAST

When you think you are doing everything right, and still your line wafts around unsteadily and falls in curves and slants rather than in a straight line to your target, you may have a case of the "slanty wobbles." Look at your reel. As it rides back and forth on the track, the only part that should ever face the fish is your line. Are you letting the rod twist so that the fish can see the face of your reel? Use your coaching hand to keep your reel straight. As your coaching hand rides along the imaginary bicycle rim, it will also straighten your cast.

CONCENTRATION

During every part of the cast, it is important to concentrate on what you are doing. Be sure to give the cast your total attention. Do not cast until you have mentally settled yourself. Are you sure what your target is? You do not want to cast blindly. Look first to see if there is a fish out there working, and think where you want your line and your fly in relation to where you think the fish is or will be.

FALSE CASTS

Do not do any unnecessary false casting—waving the rod back and forth without actually sending the line all the way out. The more you false cast, the greater the odds that something will go wrong with your final cast. And when you are fishing, that extra motion of a false cast may alert the fish. Aim for economy of movement so that you will not wear out your arm.

False casting is appropriate if you need to dry your fly, to get out more line, to measure the distance to your target, or to cancel out a misdirected cast. When you see that your fly is not going quite where you want it, about to hang up on a log right by a terrific spot where you

know there's a fish, you can pull back in a false cast before your fly and leader hit the water. Then try again to put that fly exactly where you want it.

STEP 1. ON TRACK
Taking the time to build the preparatory first step into your mental image will pay big dividends. This is the stage of the cast where you will use different approaches once you get to advanced casting. With this mental count already in place, you will have nothing to unlearn, and the extra mental effort of starting on track will help eliminate any warp in that imaginary bicycle wheel.

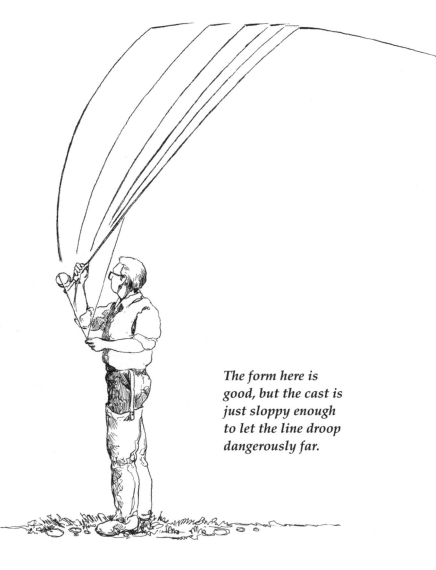

*The form here is
good, but the cast is
just sloppy enough
to let the line droop
dangerously far.*

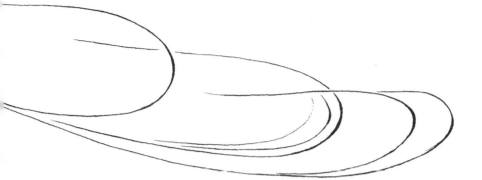

STEP 2. BACK CAST

Look up. As soon as you see the end of your line snaking into view and quickly passing overhead on its way back behind you, that is when you send out the command to end the back cast. We do mean the end of the line, which you can see, not the leader, which you probably cannot see. Because what you are actually throwing is the weight of the line, not the leader and fly, you do not need any leader or fly on the end of your line for casting practice. If you would like to see how the leader and fly behave during your casts, use a fly with the hook cut off or tie on a small twist of bright yarn.

That hesitation at the end of the back cast, that flick of the wrist, feels like tossing ice cubes out of a glass. This is because your arm is speeding up as you come back. Accelerate, accelerate, and as the rod nears vertical, stop your arm abruptly. Your stop should not be so vigorous that it throws a bounce into your rod and line. There is a brief pause while the end of your line unrolls behind you.

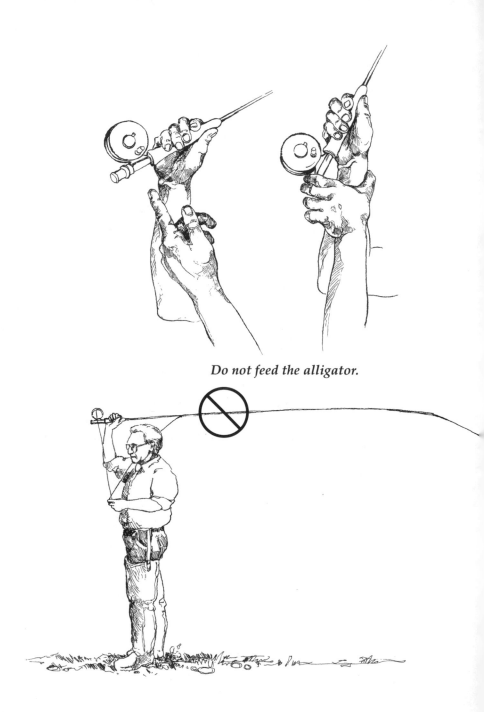

Do not feed the alligator.

CURING THE SNAPS THAT EAT YOUR FLIES

You do not want to hear any snapping sound at the back of the back cast. If you hear that dreaded snapping sound, you will probably find that you no longer have a fly on the end of your leader when it comes forward again. You should not hear a great loud swoosh as you come forward. Relax! You just want a neat, efficient, nearly soundless movement. Pay attention to your timing; don't rush.

If you hear, see, or feel your line hitting the ground behind you, you may be letting your wrist "wilt," pointing your thumb down at the ground. Try a few back casts with your free hand holding on to your casting wrist like a splint on a sprained wrist. Hook your thumb over the top of your forearm. Curl your fingers around the rod butt. Press the rod butt right against your arm. Your casting arm and wrist should feel like they have grown to be part of the rod. Try a back cast. Don't let that rod butt–forearm angle open up like the jaws of a hungry alligator. Use your coaching hand to keep those jaws almost shut. You should not be able to fit three fingers in that angle. When you have the feel of keeping the alligator jaws closed, take away your coaching hand. Now feel that you are using a slight pressure of your pinkie, ring, and middle fingers to keep those jaws nearly shut.

If you don't hear a snapping sound or find your line dropping on the ground behind you, your timing is right and you are not breaking your wrist too much. You are doing a neat, energetic, but not stiff motion. Now just do that set of motions in a perfect mirror image for the fore or delivery cast.

STEP 3. STOP. PAUSE

When you stop back there at one o'clock, do not immediately begin moving your rod forward, but hesitate. During this brief pause, your line continues backward and unrolls behind you. This is the hesitation. Let that line continue to flow backward—but not your rod.

STEP 4. FORE CAST

Now move your rod and arm forward. As the body of your line starts to pull forward, you will feel the weight of the line loading the rod. If you wait until you feel this to start forward, however, you will have waited too long, and your line will fall behind you.

On this forward motion, you accelerate at the last moment, completing your forward cast with a burst of energy from your wrist at the very last instant. Think about running to step into an elevator just before the doors close. If you started running from way back, you'd find yourself crashing into people. The same thing happens with your line.

People used to say that the forward cast is like driving a nail with a hammer. Well, don't just let the weight of the hammer hit the nail. Drive the nail, but not so hard that the hammer bounces. You don't want to bounce the rod or line. Think *speed*, not power. Don't overdo the speed at the very beginning of the hammer blow. You need to accelerate, accelerate. When you hammer your rod out and stop, it transfers the energy to the line. If you use the hammer image, it matters where you think the nail is. Picture it at about ten o'clock, just above that mirror image spot where the final acceleration is going to happen.

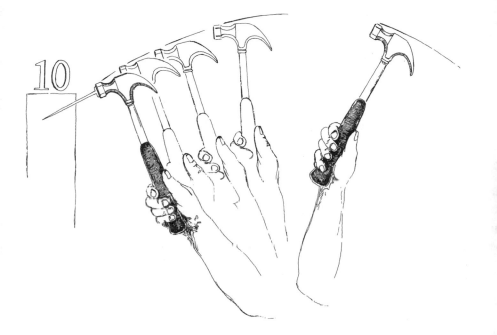

Think speed, not power.

TAILING LOOPS

If the tail end of the line collides with the part of the line closest to your rod when you are coming forward with your delivery cast, we say that you have made a tailing loop. This is a very common casting problem. People often call the resulting snarl a wind knot, but if you consider carefully, you may find that the real cause is a tailing loop. Here are some ways this problem comes about and several things you can do to avoid it.

The most common cause of a tailing loop is stopping your rod tip dead on the completion of the forward stroke. At this point you must immediately lower the rod tip slightly. Beware the natural tendency to drop your rod tip so much that it opens your casting loop. *Slightly* is the key word.

Several other errors cause tailing loops. On the back cast, the trajectory of your line may be so weak that the line starts to collapse behind you. Keep your back cast firm and high

enough so that after your hesitation, your line does not die behind you before you begin your fore cast.

You might be casting too hard too soon in the forward stroke. Apply your power and speed gradually and smoothly. When your casting stroke is stopped too short, a tailing loop might result. Lengthen your casting stroke. You might get tailing loops from casting in an erratic or jerky fashion. Apply more speed and less power during acceleration, making your approach to the completion of the cast more smooth and constant. Casting so hard that you cause a shock wave will drive the front end of your line under the main part of your line. Concentrate more on line speed, stop your rod tip smoothly, and follow through by lowering the rod tip slightly.

How do you apply only the amount of acceleration you really need? And how do you control what happens at the end of your forward acceleration? Let's take a look at what we'll call the "zing."

ZING!

Try a delivery or fore cast with your coaching hand going along for a free ride on the imaginary bicycle rim. Just at the moment you approach the ten o'clock spot, give a quick pull down with that rim hand. This will give you the proper feeling of a last-minute surge of acceleration. It will most assuredly teach you the wonderful feeling of zinging that line out there! As you did at one o'clock with the alligator jaws, take away the coaching hand. This time apply slight pressure with your casting hand pinkie, ring, and middle fingers. Now you will feel, at the moment of this ten o'clock stop, that you are showing your thumbnail to the ten o'clock spot out there on the imaginary clock face. You are tossing the ice cubes from that imaginary glass in the direction of the ten o'clock spot. This slight, zingy, finger pressure that lowers your rod tip ever so slightly will keep your leader and hook from tangling on the trip forward in that dreaded tailing loop.

Your free hand helps control the line during the last part of the cast as the line is flowing forward.

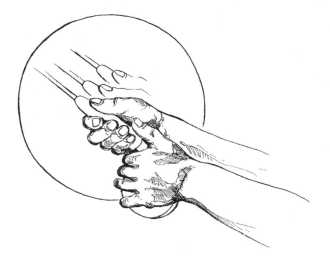

When you approach the ten o'clock spot on the imaginary bicycle rim, give a quick pull with the rim hand.

STEP 5. FISH THROUGH

After you have made your fore cast, transfer your line to the rod hand and promptly take care of any slack. The thumb on your free hand and the forefinger have formed a circle, or donut, into which the line has slipped. You could think of your free hand as the first rod guide. This is how you lightly control the line during the last part of the cast. This way your line cannot flip and flap and wrap itself around your rod and reel.

When your fly settles perfectly on target, you want to be ready for a strike, with your line under control. Your line should be in direct and sensitive connection with your fly so that you can feel the strike and set it with the proper firm but delicate lift. By having lowered your rod tip to point at the water, you have given yourself some striking distance to use when setting the hook. The fish will likely be facing upstream, so to set the hook, give a little stab downcurrent or use a small pulse up toward the sky, Statue of Liberty style. You don't want to pull the fly out of the fish's mouth.

THE SLIP STRIKE

The slip strike is a neat little trick that builds in a shock absorber, allowing some tension on the line, but not so much that you break off a big fish because you can't react quickly enough to give him a little line. Allow a little extra line, just 4 or 5 inches, between the reel and your braking hand on the rod butt. As you lift the rod to set the hook, let that extra line slip through your braking fingers. Use this valuable move on both saltwater giants and little brookies, and you will hook more fish.

If you are fishing for bass any other hard-mouthed fish, instead of using the slip strike, give your line a good pull with your free hand to set the hook. When that big bass hits, use your rod tip as a shock absorber and a lever.

CASTING AT OTHER ANGLES

When you are comfortable with these steps, try canting the imaginary wheel—slanting it away from the vertical. If the wind is blowing your fly toward your face, or a bush is standing right where you need to back cast, you may want to alter your casting procedure by canting your rod.

The bicycle wheel principle still holds. Do not warp the wheel. Practice with the imaginary wheel canted out away from your body to cast under the wind or under an overhanging branch. Practice casting vertically as you usually do, and then cast with your rod canted across in front of your body. Your free hand should "go along for the ride" to eliminate warp and wobble till you get the feel of doing each position accurately.

THE ROLL CAST

There are often times when you simply do not have room for a back cast. A tree or bush or other obstacle stands right behind you. Roll cast to the rescue. For this cast, you need to do your practicing on the water.

Begin the roll cast with some line out on the water. Hold the rod tip low. Now bring your rod up toward you, gliding the line across the water. Come to a complete stop as soon as the rod passes slightly behind you. The instant your line stops and you feel surface tension gripping your line, complete your forward cast. You absolutely need to stop and wait for the surface tension to give your rod something to pull against. Then complete your forward cast as you would with a normal cast.

THE LONG OR DIFFICULT CASTS

On long or difficult casts, such as casting into the wind or casting heavy flies, use your whole arm and whatever body motion is necessary to reach way back behind you. Make a much larger, flatter arc than the short-cast bike wheel; picture your reel hand going for a long ride on a wagon wheel. Cant the rod and your arm approaching the horizontal. You are describing more than a 90-degree arc, perhaps close to 180 degrees. You don't cast harder or faster; you just reach back farther. For a 60-foot cast your rod might move back to about one thirty on the clock face. For a 90-foot cast, you might take it clear back to three o'clock. You should still keep your motions as economical as possible. Don't ever work any harder than you have to at casting. You want to be able to do it all day long!

The first time you decide to work out more line to throw a longer cast, you will probably wind up with a mess. Since this is most likely to happen at the end of what was a good casting session, reel in and wait for another day. Even thinking about

really powering that line out there is likely to mess up your
timing. You begin the hammer blow acceleration too soon,
and plow into your own line coming forward. Just get a grip
on yourself and pay close attention to the count. Carefully
watch your line overhead. As you back cast, a longer length
of line naturally takes more time to come flying overhead.
Wait till you actually see the end of it for that back stop, pause.
Wait till you see it come forward in the mirror image delivery,
fore cast. Then follow through.

THE NEXT STEP

This is a simple framework for understanding casting. You will constantly be making adjustments according to weather conditions, the action of the rod you are using, your physical state, and even your mood. As soon as people see you with a rod in your hand, they will probably try to give you advice. Think about what they are trying to tell you. Maybe they are describing what you have just learned, only using different words. Use the advice that fits you and let the rest slip quietly by. You know what a cast should look like. You know how to count through the five steps. You know how a good cast feels. Put your free hand on the reel to steady that bike wheel if you find that your casts are getting wobbly. Practice, practice, practice!

Consult the master casters. Read the columns of Joan Salvato Wulff and, especially if you are casting for bass, Dave Whitlock and Harry Murray. Check out Doug Swisher's educated, microsecond wrist and track explanations in his tapes and writings. Read Ed Jaworoski, check out Mel Krieger, and review Lefty Kreh's tapes and books, especially regarding getting the line in motion and using your whole arm in the long-distance cast. Bear in mind that experts don't always do exactly what they say. Watch the video images for yourself. You will see that most expert casters use the bicycle wheel motion in combination with the grooved track image. Then visualize yourself doing it. See it, say it, do it!

Consult your local Orvis fly shop or telephone the Orvis toll-free number, (800) 235-9763, for information on Orvis fly-casting schools.

PHYSICAL CHALLENGES

We all have limitations. How do we deal with physical challenges? Here are some suggestions for knots and procedures that will benefit everyone. Since you are reading this guide, you probably have enough motivation, perseverance, and ingenuity to figure out how to adjust the casting procedure to your particular needs. Once you thoroughly understand the bicycle wheel concept, you will be able to figure out how to do what is essential.

Let's look at the casting procedure.

The Grip

How is your hand built? Trust your own intuition to work out a grip that gives you maximum control with minimum effort. If you arm performance is limited, you will find that the two-handed cast is your best friend.

The Arc

Learn the 90-degree arc between ten and one o'clock. Think creatively. Perhaps you can't cast holding the rod out to either side of your body. If a midline position is all that is available to you, that will work. Bring the rod back as far as your forehead. Stop. That may not give you quite enough space for a full 90-degree quarter of a circle, but that's okay. Just be sure you stick with the ten o'clock position for the forward stop.

Keep in mind that you can cant the bicycle wheel in any direction as long as you don't warp the rim. If you are using two hands, you may be limited by the reach of that second hand. Do whatever is necessary so that the second hand can come along to help.

The Stance

Don't hesitate to modify the stance to your own needs. If you are in a wheelchair, you won't be able to shift your weight to help you propel the cast, but you'll probably find that the two-handed cast works fine. Cant the bike wheel to any angle you need.

John loves the sound of the water playing around his waterproof wheels.

The Cast

Don't try to work with more line than you can control. That will just frustrate your progress. Honor every single step of the count, particularly step 5. Fish the cast all the way through.

Probably part of the reason you wanted to learn fly casting is because it looks so lovely and free. We all have mental images of long, sweeping false casts. But remember, you usually don't need to false cast. Conserve your energy so that you can cast all day long.

Paul uses a push-button reel to take up line and is especially careful to fish a short line. He has modified his casting style only slightly. He brings his one arm to his forehead rather than back to one o'clock. Then he powers the rod out to the ten o'clock position for neat, accurate casts.

In the interest of preserving the sense of independence, solitude, and liberation that fly fishing offers, you may prefer not to use special harnesses, potentially balky automatic reels, and the like. Most answers lie within yourself. Concentrate on conserving all the energy inherent in the bicycle wheel. You will learn to read the water well so that long casts are not necessary. Learn to use the hand twist retrieve (see page 58). Use your lips and teeth if you have to. Use a stripping basket to collect your line if that helps. If necessary, wedge the rod between your legs, under the stump of a limb, or into a Velcro holder sewn on your vest. Do whatever works for you.

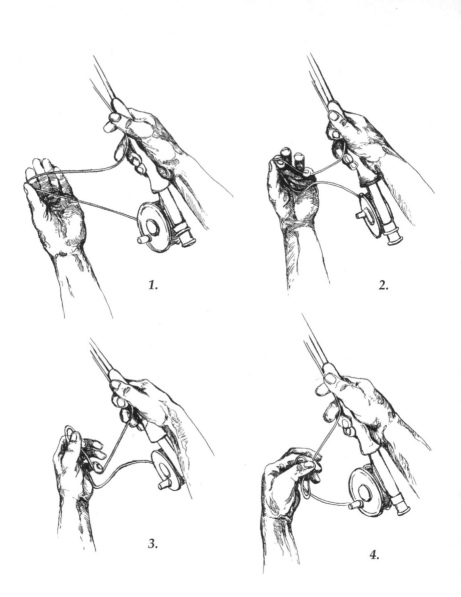

The hand twist retrieve. With a small rocking motion of your hand, let your fingers gather the line in a loose, twisting retrieve. Your personal variation of this slow, constant retrieve is an excellent action to make your nymph or fly move at a natural pace.

Changing Flies and Leaders

You're inevitably going to lose flies, snagging them in the trees overhead or on rocks and logs underwater. That means you have to know how to tie on flies and replace lost leader. If you don't have two deft hands, changing flies and leaders may present a special challenge. Normally you tie the tippet (the section of the leader material that attaches to the fly) onto the leader with a surgeon's knot. It's convenient to use leaders that connect to your line by a loop fitted through the loop you have built into the end of your fly line.

You could also make up flies already tied on tippet. If you fashion a loop in the end of the tippet, the loop-to-loop connection is simple. But keeping flies and lengths of tippet unsnarled is not simple. You would probably do better to learn to tie a modified clinch knot with one hand (see page 62).

If you have nimble fingers but your eyesight is poor, you can use special magnifiers and hooks with large eyes. You could also learn to tie the Swisher version of the turle knot (see page 60). Once you get the hang of it, you can tie it quickly without looking at it. As with any knot, try it first with some line that is large enough to be cooperative.

Practice, practice, practice tying knots before you go out on the water, and review your skills before the start of every season.

1.

2.

3.

A Knot You Can Learn to Tie by Feel

Tying this knot is like tying chain crochet. To tie it, put the tippet down through the eye of the fly and slide the fly several inches along the butt, or line end, of the tippet. Next, form a slip knot around the right hand while holding the tag end of the tippet in the left hand. To do this, make a loop around the fingers of the right hand as shown (1). Pull your left hand holding the tippet tag toward you and rotate your right hand, little finger down (2). Your right thumb and forefinger will grasp the tippet between the loop and the fly. Reach out (3) and pull a few inches of tippet back through the loop, thus forming a new loop—the slip knot, or crochet chain—around the right hand, all the time holding onto the tag end with your left hand.

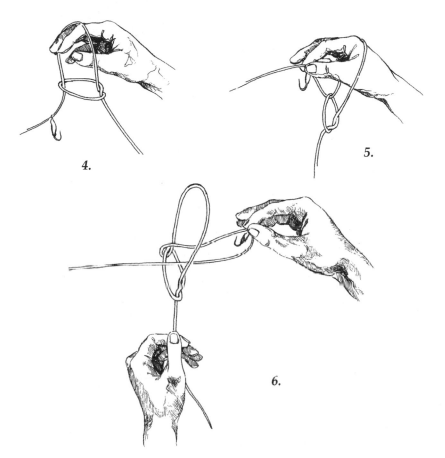

4.

5.

6.

Now reach through the big loop of the slip knot with the thumb and forefinger of the right hand, grasp the fly, and put it through the loop. Tighten the tag end with the left hand and snug the slip knot down against the eye of the fly. Trim the tag end.

With practice, this modified version of Doug Swisher's swirle knot can be tied entirely by feel.

A Clinch Knot for One Hand

Secure the fly by hooking it into a short-sheared fleece pad on your vest, a tree branch, or your rod butt cork. You could clamp the fly at the hook bend in forceps, which you then rest on your lap or hold with your knees or even your feet. Maintaining tension on the line from the rod may be a challenge.

Thread the tag end of the tippet through the eye of the fly. The large eyes of Orvis Big Eye Hooks make threading easier. To make tying easier, give yourself 3 or 4 inches of tag to work with. Fold the tag back along the tippet. With a rolling movement of your thumb and fore-finger, work the tag end around the leader five complete twists. Bend the tag end back toward the eye of the fly and pass the tag through the first loop by the eye. (If you can manage it, try the popular modification known as the improved clinch knot that calls for you to pass the tag through the loop farthest from the eye as well.)

Hold the tag so that it does not slip out of the loop and pull the fly. Too much tension on the tag end will cause the knot to tighten incorrectly. In either case, use a generous length of leader so that you can maneuver and see what you are doing. After you pull tight, trim off the excess. Experiment and see what works best for you.

RODS

It is inevitable that a book about learning how to cast drifts into learning how to fish. You may have borrowed this book and you may have borrowed a rod. Now that you are really hooked, you should buy your own copy of this book and a rod.

The weight of line you throw determines what weight rod you need. Rods are usually rated for a weight of line, and lines are built in a variety of tapers. In addition to the type of weather, water, and fish, the size of the fly most often determines what weight line you need. So what size fly do you need? If you are going to fish for bass or other large game fish, you want to be able to cast a hefty fly. Think about an 8-weight rod and line. To cast that, you might like all the leverage of a 9-foot rod. The extra length may also come in handy for dapping your fly into a clear space in the weeds. If you are fishing a very short line because of a physical handicap, you may find the long rod helpful. Try the rod out to be sure it is pleasant to use. You don't want to wear yourself out waving a heavy, stiff clunker around all day.

The rod you use for large bass flies may also be just what you need for tossing out large saltwater flies. If you buy a good-quality reel, it is likely to be corrosion resistant. You need only stand your rod in the shower after fishing to wash the salt off rod, reel, and line.

Suppose you plan on going after trout. On a big western river on a windy day, you may want a hefty rod. But if it's a gorgeous windless day and you'd like to feel every ounce of the fight, you might enjoy challengingly light tackle. If your idea of fun is creeping through alders in the East after wild brookies, you probably want something even lighter and shorter. How short? There is no such thing as a rod short enough to carry through alders without getting hung up, so get a rod long enough to feel good when you cast with it, probably around 7 feet.

What weight rod should you choose? Rods that throw a 4-, 5-, or 6-weight line are considered middle-of-the-road. Suppose you want to cast tiny midges, say size 20-something. And suppose the fish you tie into are not very heavy; maybe they are scrappy little panfish. You'll have a lot of fun if you use an ultralight rod, which can be as light as a 1-weight. If you use a very light rod, you'll need to think about not playing the fish to exhaustion if you plan to release it.

By now it should be obvious that it would be great to have a whole wardrobe of rods so that you always have the right one for the size fly, the size fish, the force of the wind, and the space available between the bushes. So any single rod you buy will be a compromise. And as you become more proficient, your preference will likely change from one rod action to another.

Action is how and where the rod bends—at the tip with a quick rebound, slowly all the way to the butt with a slow rebound, or something in between. The graphite rod is the top choice for most of today's anglers, as it is strongest, lightest, and most responsive. Some people prefer the traditional grace and beauty of the bamboo rod, however, which is expensive and offers a slow, delicate action. Glass rods are durable and the least expensive. Which is best? It's really a matter of personal preference.

To buy the right rod, you also need to talk with knowledgeable sales staff. The advice provided in this book is meant to give you some basic knowledge so that you can carry on a decent conversation with someone who knows what he or she is talking about. Go to a fishing shop or, if that is not possible, talk with the experts at the catalog companies—not the person who is trained merely to take down your phone order. They are great fun to talk with and will help you sort out your needs. If you are a serious fisherman, buy the best rod you can afford. Keep in mind that you usually get what you pay for, but you don't need the most expensive rod to cast a fly.

ETIQUETTE

You will learn quickly that your peers do not appreciate you thundering by, close to the edge of the water, putting down all the fish. Ask other anglers whether they are intending to fish upstream or down, and don't cut in ahead of them. Ask something like, "Do you mind if I go up a hundred yards or so?" How wide a berth they expect you to give them depends on what region of the country you are in, but it should go without saying that you need to be at least far enough away that your line does not cross theirs.

FISHING COMPANIONS

It's pleasant to have companionship while fishing, and on the drive to the fishing spot as well. You need not feel shy about finding a fishing companion. Most experienced anglers love to share their knowledge. They know that as a novice, you stand to learn a lot from more experienced fishermen. Knowledge, like beauty, becomes even more precious when it is shared.

For anyone around water, it's wise to use the buddy system so that someone else knows where you are. You and your companion alternate fishing the good holes as you make your way upstream. Ideally, your partner is not too close to you, just barely in touch.

How do you find a fishing companion? Why not join the local chapter of an organization like Trout Unlimited or the Federation of Fly Fishers? Call or write the national office for more information.

Trout Unlimited
800 Follin Lane, S.E., Suite 250
Vienna, VA 22180-4959
(703) 522-0200

Federation of Fly Fishers
Box 1595
502 South 19th Avenue
Bozeman, MT 59758
(406) 585-7592

THE MOST COMMON CASTING MISTAKES

Ask yourself the following questions before and after every casting practice session. Look back at the appropriate topic in the coaching tips section for advice on how to correct these common mistakes.

1. Are you trying to cast too much line?
2. Are you starting into your back cast with the rod tip held too high?
3. Are you breaking your wrist too much on the back cast?
4. Are you working too hard at casting, making your motions too vigorously?
5. Are you letting your forearm ride up too high above your shoulder when you reach back on the back cast?

Be honest with yourself. You need a strong desire to learn to cast. You cannot do it just to please someone else. When you are really ready, you CAN learn.

THE END

Now you're pointed in the right direction. You've learned to be your own coach. You have learned how to cast well enough to enjoy fishing, look for a rod, find fishing partners, and practice etiquette on the stream.

Learning to cast is only one of the steps in learning to fish. Books, videos, and fly-fishing magazines will teach you such skills as water reading and fly selection and use. You will learn to catch and, equally important, you will learn how to release fish properly. We hope you will also learn to become an environmental ambassador for all our waters and the life therein.

Happy fishing!

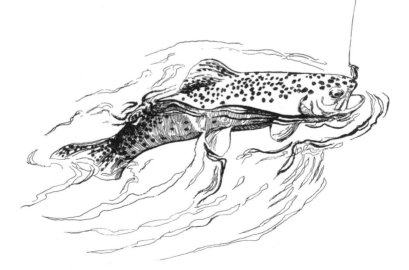

Afterword

by Peter H. McNair

This book is intended to be a simple, concise guide to casting for anyone who wants to learn to fly fish. In days gone by, you probably would have learned to cast from a mentor. Today you can learn from a book, such as this one, a video, or a fly-casting clinic, but there are things about the general development and evolution of fly fishing that most of these sources will not teach you.

I have been fly fishing in Montana since the 1950s. Some of the changes I've seen in fly fishing over the years are not pleasant, but others give cause for optimism. Because my dad and I were friends of Norman Maclean, I especially delight in sharing the story of the restoration of the Big Blackfoot River, as an example of both the accomplishments and the challenges facing fly fishing today.

Around the time the movie based on Norman's wonderful book *A River Runs through It* was released, the Orvis Company joined with Trout Unlimited in a project to restore the Blackfoot River to some semblance of what it had been in the days when Norman and my father fished it, about seventy-five years ago. Orvis announced a tollfree number for people to use to contribute to the project and was overwhelmed with the response. Additional phone lines were needed as support poured in. Nobody had anticipated such an outpouring of enthusiasm for fly fishing. And it shows no signs of abating.

Let's take a closer look at the phenomenon. The filming of *A River Runs through It*, which popularized and publicized Maclean's book, engrossed the whole town of Bozeman, Montana, where I live. Because the Blackfoot had been so severely degraded by a combination of careless mining practices and unbridled timber harvesting, this once magnificent river—one of the main characters in the book—could not be used in the filming of the movie. Instead, parts of five other rivers around the region were used for the filming.

Much of the footage was shot on the West Gallatin River, which my neighbor and coauthor Gary Lewis and I consider to be our home waters. The Gallatin has to be one of the comeliest stretches of river anywhere in the world. From its sources in the wilderness snowfields of northwest Yellowstone National Park, the Gallatin meanders pastorally through high-mountain moose meadows, roars and rushes through cliff-bordered canyons, and then seductively opens into the broad Valley of Flowers to join the Madison and Jefferson rivers, becoming in turn the mighty Missouri.

The Blackfoot lies farther north and west than its stand-in, the Gallatin. The Blackfoot is born on the crest of the Continental Divide. Here, at Rogers Pass, was recorded the lowest temperature ever in the continental United States, over 70 degrees below zero Fahrenheit. Ice age temperatures and ice age forces carved the Blackfoot. Glaciers dominate its soul. Cold waters thread through graceful alpine meadows and warm as they negotiate logjams, gravel bars, and rugged canyons to reach the confluence a hundred miles downstream at the Clark Fork.

Norman lived to see the decline of the Blackfoot, and it troubled him. If he were alive today, he would be pleased with the improvements brought about by the cooperative efforts of a number of dedicated people. The Blackfoot had been in decline for a number of years. Many people failed to see how their individual actions were having a cumulative effect. Even Mother Nature seemed to have abandoned the Big Blackfoot as years of extreme drought contributed to the decline of the river. Finally the problems became so obvious the Big Blackfoot could not even pass a screen test for its own part. As Becky Garland, president of the Blackfoot chapter of Trout Unlimited would say, the Big Blackfoot had been overmined, overrecreated, overfished, overagricultured, overlogged, and overlooked by everyone.

The Blackfoot chapter of Trout Unlimited decided to take on what seemed to almost everyone else to be too big a problem. Working tirelessly for more than ten years, they put together a coalition of a number of agencies, landowners, individuals, and corporations. With funding from Orvis and a number of individuals, they were able to initiate a baseline study. Data gathered by the Montana Fish, Wildlife and Parks Department would now replace the old memories and fish stories to provide a real basis for change. The bulk of the restoration work was done not on the Big Blackfoot itself; it was the tributaries that proved key to the rehabilitation of the waterway. They are the bedroom areas for fish and the source of the Blackfoot's nutrients. There has been an amazing increase, more than 100 percent, in redd (spawning beds) and fry (hatched fish) counts throughout the ecosystem. The Fish, Wildlife and Parks Department has also changed the regulations for the river. There are now size and number limits on the take of rainbows, and the native cutthroat and bull trout are strictly catch-and-release.

The restoration of the Big Blackfoot is a remarkable tale of cooperation among individuals, companies, and organizations such as Trout Unlimited, the Montana Fish, Wildlife and Parks Department, the U.S. Fish and Wildlife Service, the Bureau of Land Management, the Water Quality Bureau, and the Soil Conservation Service. The real magic of this process is that the

very interests and industries that had contributed to the problem were those that contributed to the solution. This local coalition has received an astonishing outpouring of support from all across the country.

The Big Blackfoot success story has inspired the Orvis Company to continue its efforts, donating 6 percent of its gross profits on sales to The Nature Conservancy, the country's largest private conservation organization. Begun in the 1950s by ecologists, The Nature Conservancy has remained dedicated to securing environmental protection for significant ecosystems. The Nature Conservancy has been remarkably successful at involving both corporations and members of a broad spectrum of the general public. It is recognized that people are a part of the ecosystems but that natural lands have a value in and of themselves. To the angler standing in the rushing waters of Montana's premier trout waters, this is a persuasive proposition.

Montana's Fish, Wildlife and Parks Department, with the help of many dedicated fishermen like Becky Garland and Gary Lewis, has introduced management tactics that maxi-

mize the fishing potential of our habitats. Granted, Montana is spectacularly endowed, but other states are now seeing the wisdom of the type of special regulations and research programs that Montana has had in place for years.

A key concept in Montana's fishery management is that of catch-and-release. One of my favorite mentors was my uncle, Mickey McNair. When Uncle Mickey was growing up in Montana, the state required kids to stay in school through eighth grade. Release came none too soon for Mickey, who at age fourteen became a woodsman. He grew to be a great outdoorsman, fur trapper, and naturalist. Though he always believed that one could and should use the gifts of nature and earth, he also knew that resources were finite. He taught me the concept of respect for ecosystems and to leave the environment as undisturbed as possible. He was one of the first to teach me to leave fish, berries, and all living things with the ability to continue to be fruitful and multiply.

Today's angler may envy the stories of old-timers about how many baskets of fish they caught in one day. The sizzling, fish-filled skillet over the blazing campfire is a most delectable image. And for sure, a kid may not want to let that first-ever fish go back to mysteries of the watery deeps. But gradually the modern angler evolves to the point where killing the fish does not seem an important part of the process of fishing.

To practice catch-and-release, fish with barbless hooks or simply bend down the barb of any hook with fishing pliers. Then you will be able to remove the fish from the hook quickly and gently. You may think that using barbless hooks will mean fewer fish caught, but you will find that this is not the case.

Although studies seem to show that damage from barbed or multiple hooks is one of the highest causes of fish mortality, you should also be careful not to overplay fish. You know that the fish was likely to swallow the whole hook if you have ever fished with worms. As a fly fisher, you have the responsibility to judge how long to play the fish (unless the fish outwits you and arranges its own long-distance release!). After you have set the hook with that slight rising motion, adrenaline takes over, and you find yourself in a moment you wish could last forever; however, you really should bring the fish in for release promptly, well before stressful conditions overpower the fish. This presupposes that you have thoughtfully chosen an adequate tippet strength. If your situation requires the use of weights, use the new nontoxic, nonlead fishing weights.

To land a fish, use a net with a soft mesh, and do not keep the fish out of water any longer than absolutely necessary. Handle the fish with care. Avoid squeezing it. Promptly place the fish, upright, back in its waters and release it. If the fish is slow in recovering, hold its head pointing upcurrent, cradling its body just under the surface of the water. Let the water circulate through its gills by gently moving the fish up and downstream until it recovers and can swim back out into the current on its own. If you have been fortunate enough to catch a really large fish, you may find that grasping it with one hand just in front of the tail and the other near the pectoral fins is the best way to hold it. You will get great satisfaction watching the lovely creature disappear back into the safety of its haunts to be caught again another day.

These days everyone is talking about whirling disease, an introduced waterborne parasite from Europe that has spread rapidly in the past ten years. Unfortunately, it is far from the only threat of its kind. Let's take a look at introductions. Did

you know that our brown trout are descended from imports from Germany? And rainbows were originally native only west of the Rockies. Zebra mussels and whirling disease are teaching us that many introductions do not prove so benign.

All of us can take an active role in preventing the spread of aquatic pathogens like whirling disease. Here are a few common precautionary measures that should be a part of all fishing routines: Clean and dry all of your equipment every time you go fishing—your boat, canoe, or float tube as well as your waders. Resist the temptation to transport any species of fish to stock another body of water. It's not only ecologically unwise, but it is illegal in most states as well. The same applies to the transport of streamside and aquatic plants, no matter how attractive you may find them. It is a difficult lesson, but often our environments are best left as they are. We humans do not yet know enough ecology to run the natural world better that it runs itself!

As an evolving ecologist, you will want to learn to recognize redds, tributary conditions, stresses, and sources of pollution. You will not fish on those days when the very warmth of the water places undue stress on the fish. For the new and experienced angler alike, becoming well informed and sensitive to a broad range of political and environmental issues is essential and fascinating. If you observe that some practices are perfectly legal but nevertheless are damaging, you may wish to join others to get protective regulations improved where you fish. New allies are to be found all around you. A wide variety of groups now recognize the importance of water quality and riparian issues.

You will also find your own sense of personal responsibility evolving. Gary carries with him a plastic trash bag. On the way back to the vehicle, he gives his clients the quiet example of one man's cleanup campaign. Guides on Grand Canyon raft trips now have no trouble convincing their clients to cooperate in body waste carryout policies, which represent a fairly major change in attitude but only a minor inconvenience. More and more campers observe a no-fires policy. We can expect ever-evolving practices for coexisting with our lovely natural world, and we can all help shape those practices and attitudes.

I was one of the most fortunate boys growing up in the fifites and early sixties, as I had a number of good books and friends to teach me both techniques and values. Whether we have learned from a book, or from people, we can all become mentors. We can dedicate ourselves to learning and passing on our knowledge. We are not powerless. Everyone who fishes can make a difference to the future of fly fishing.

Because we are living entities, water surges through our bodies, making us kin to the rivers and waters we love. Hydrologic cycles, and all the grand and small cycles of life and death affect each one of us. We are forced to become ecologists. Norman Maclean said he was haunted by waters. Aren't we all?

GARY LEWIS

Montana native Gary Lewis was inspired to take up fly fishing by his dad and encouraged by his good friend and fishing partner of many years Jim Stevens. Gary spent five years as a paratrooper with the 82nd Airborne Division after playing baseball a year for the Billings Mustangs, farm team of the Brooklyn Dodgers. He has been an avid handball player for many years. For the past thirty-eight years, Gary has been fly fishing in his home state, Idaho, and Wyoming. He has taught fishing and fly tying, and eight years ago assumed the post of fly-fishing program director at Lone Mountain Ranch, an Orvis-endorsed lodge at Big Sky, Montana.

Gary was an early member of both the Federation of Fly Fishers and Trout Unlimited and has given support to special projects such as fish censuring and stream-improvement projects.

A soft-spoken gentleman, Gary quietly goes about innovating. He never claims inventions, but years ago he had an idea for gluing carpet fibers onto wader soles. The search for the perfect nonslip, durable material led him to consult several chemical and fishing equipment companies, and the rest is felt sole history. From elements of vest design to early hiring of women as guides and offering youth clinics and women-only days, Gary continues to expand the frontiers of fly fishing. His love for winter fly fishing has now led to year-round guiding operations at Big Sky. Gary and his wife, Georgiann, reside in Bozeman.

MARNIE REED CROWELL

Author Marnie Reed Crowell attended Randolph-Macon Woman's College and received an M.S. in biology from the University of Pennsylvania. When she's not fishing in Montana, she considers Penobscot Bay, Maine, where she has summered for many years, and the Ausable and St. Lawrence rivers in New York her home waters.

Her writings have appeared in such magazines as *Reader's Digest*, *Redbook*, and *Natural History*. Her books include *North to St. Lawrence*, a history of New York's North Country that was made into a three-part television series; *Greener Pastures*, a chronicle of rural living published by Funk & Wagnalls; and *Great Blue, The Odyssey of a Heron*, published by Times Books, the story of a heron's migration from Maine to the Caribbean.

Marnie has hosted a national storytelling series for National Public Radio. She serves on the Board of Trustees of Kneisel Hall Chamber Music School and Festival, and of the Island Heritage Trust. She is a steward for The Nature Conservancy and currently serves as a director of the St. Lawrence Valley chapter of Trout Unlimited.

Creator and owner of the list server MISTNET (Migration Information School Tracking NETwork), linking birders and students throughout the Americas, Marnie also wrote an early home page on the World Wide Web on the Internet. She teaches a course on environmental responsibility for the First-Year Program at St. Lawrence University.

PETER H. McNAIR

At the age of seventeen, the young outdoorsman and naturalist Peter McNair was catching arctic char and lake trout on a fly in the Canadian Arctic Islands. He was assisting his father, a Dartmouth geologist who, like his Montana friend Norman Maclean, had gone east to seek his fortune.

After attending college at St. Lawrence University and doing graduate work in ecology at the University of Montana, Peter was a forest firefighter, commercial fisherman, fisheries biologist, photographer, and teacher in Alaska and Montana. He started the Bozeman Bureau of KTVM-TV in Montana and became general manager of KIEM-TV in Eureka, California, where he lent his considerable energies to a number of community and conservation efforts, including the Cal-Or Steelhead Rehabilitation project. He designed the Firehole fishing vest for Bridger Designs.

Long an advocate for sustainable use resources and wild lands, Peter has worked for the Sierra Club and Wilderness Society, and is a supporter of Trout Unlimited, Ducks Unlimited, the Great Bear Foundation, and the Clark Museum Foundation. He has taught sciences, environmental education, outdoor recreation, and special education, and for many years served on the board of directors for Montana Public Television. A former national alpine champion and professional ski racer, Peter shares his expertise by coaching both alpine and nordic skiing, as well as soccer and mountain climbing.

Peter now makes his home in Bozeman, where he shares the beauties of Montana with his children, Ingrid and Andy, introducing them to the joys of fishing.

ROBERT SPANNRING

Montana wildlife artist Robert Spannring makes his home on a ranch in Paradise Valley outside Livingston, Montana, where he was born and raised. A painter and illustrator, he studied ceramics and printmaking at Montana State University in Bozeman. Fishing, hunting, and camping have always been part of his life. In recent years he has bicycled across much of the West and camped in Europe. His daughter Suzanna is starting to join him streamside.

His works have been published in *Letters from Yellowstone* (Robert Rinehart Publishers); *Field Guide to Grizzly Bears* (Sasquatch Books); *North Face of Yellowstone* (Western States Publishers); the Greater Yellowstone Coalition's *An Environmental Profile of the Greater Yellowstone Ecosystem;* the Montana Department of Fish, Wildlife & Parks magazine *Montana Outdoors;* and *Bugle,* the magazine of the Rocky Mountain Elk Foundation. He has also done work for the United States Forest Service and Defenders of Wildlife and recently produced an eighteen-foot acrylic painting of a streambed, a floor piece for educating anglers.

Robert's work focuses on wildlife, its habitat, and the monumental landscapes that occupy the minds of most westerners. His paintings, which are shown at prestigious galleries throughout the West, explore the relationship between wildife and humans and the environments they share.

Index